Crochet:

How to Crochet for Beginners:

21 Amazing Tips and Tricks for

Crochet Patterns and Stitches

SARAH MILLER

CONTENTS

SARAH MILLER

Introduction

I want to thank you and congratulate you for purchasing the book,
"How to Crochet for Beginners: 21 Amazing Tips and Tricks for
Crochet Patterns, Stitches, Hats, Bags, Flowers, Gifts, Gloves,
Scarves, and Babies."

This book contains proven steps and strategies on how to crochet
simple projects within twenty-four hours.

Before you begin the simple, one-day patterns in this book, you
should know a little more about the crochet hooks and the yarns that
you're using, as well as some of the accessories you could purchase
once you become more comfortable.

The crochet hook and yarn actually coincide with one another. The
larger the hook, the larger size yarn you'll want to use. Some crochet
hooks are so small that you should be crocheting with a thick thread,
rather than yarn. Depending on the pattern you'll be making, you
may a different sized hook; otherwise, you will end up with a piece
that is larger than you first intended. Therefore, you may want to
grab a set of hooks rather than just one, or start out with patterns you

know will coincide with the size hook you have.

In addition to the size of the hook, you need to know the size of the yarn. Smaller yarn will be used for more intricate patterns. If you decide to make a baby blanket with small yarn, you're going to spend more than a day on it. However, if you use yarn that is too large, your project will come out looking lumpy, rather than looking professional and neat.

You'll find that there is also mention of stitch markers in this book. Stitch markers are small pieces you can purchase at almost any craft store or at an online retailer's website. They can be soft, beaded, hard, or have numbers or letters on them. Here's an example of how they're used

They simply mark the beginning or the end of a row so that you know where to put your next stitch. These are especially helpful for beginners or for more intricate pieces. Some crocheters are known to make their own stitch markers. Just make sure they can be removed from the final piece, unless you want to use them for decoration, of course.

21 Amazing Tips and Tricks for Crochet Patterns, Stitches, Hats, Bags, Flowers, Gifts, Gloves, Scarves, and Babies

And that's really all you need to know to begin this book! Happy crocheting!

Thanks again for purchasing this book; I hope you enjoy it!

Chain Stitch Wrapping Ribbon

Materials

- Yarn
- Crochet hook
- Scissors

Directions

1. Add a slip knot to the hook.

2. Chain twenty-five stitches while watching the tension. Be sure the tension for the stitches is consistent.

3. Once you're finished, pull the final stitch through, and pull it tight.

Chain Stitch Necklace

Materials

- Yarn

- Crochet hook

- Scissors

- Crochet needle

Directions

1. Use three colors of yarn and blend them together as one piece of yarn. Chain one piece until you're able to wrap it around your neck four to six times. Tie the ends into a knot and use a needle to hide the ends through the piece.

Crochet Bracelet with Button

Materials

- Two colors of yarn or two skeins of one color

- Size I crochet hook

- Scissors

- Crochet needle

- Sewing thread that matches your yarn

- Sewing needle

- Buttons

Directions

1. Chain twenty-one stitches.

2. Turn the piece and skip one chain. Then single crochet in the second stitch from the end. Then single crochet nineteen stitches to the end of the first row.

3. When you're at the end, single crochet twice more into the final stitch. There are going to be three single crochet stitches in the final stitch.

4. Go around with the single crochets in an oval direction to the other end. Once you're at the end, single crochet another two stitches into the final stitch while you turn the oval around, just as you did with the first end in step number three.

5. Once you're out of the end of the oval, slip stitch to the first single crochet of that row to finish off your piece. Cut the yarn, pull it through, and hide your tails.

6. If you want to add a new color to the first finished piece, then make a slip stitch with your second piece of yarn. Put the hook through the double V-stitch of the first part anywhere along that part. Add the slip knot of the first color to the hook and pull it through. Chain one. This is going to be the first stitch in the row.

7. Keep crocheting using single crochet stitches, going through the V stitches with your second color until you get to one end.

8. Once you're at one end of the piece, chain four stitches. Skip two stitches and then single crochet the second color back into the piece.

9. Keep crocheting all the way around until you get to the
    beginning stitch.

10. Slip stitch with the second color once you come to the first
    stitch. Pull the yarn through, trim off the end, and hide the
    tail into the piece with the needle.

11. Pick out a button for the bracelet. Then thread the needle
    with a little sewing thread and tie a knot on the end of your
    thread. Sew the button to the non-hole end of the bracelet
    and sew up through the yarn, through the button, and then
    tie a knot. Do this a few times. Hide the thread through the
    piece and trim off any excess.

Crochet Bunting Necklace

Materials

- Sport weight yarn

- Size E or 3.5mm crochet hook

- Chain

- Jewelry jump rings

- Needle nose pliers

Directions

1. Chain five times.

2. Single crochet in the second chain from the hook and every remaining chain across in order to get a total of four single crochet stitches. Chain once and then turn.

3. Single crochet in your first two stitches. Then do a single crochet decrease. To do this, insert the hook into the next stitch and pull your yarn through and then there will be two loops on the hook. Don't pull the yarn through them yet. Insert the hook into the final stitch and pull the yarn through

it once more. There will be three loops on the hook that span the final two stitches of the previous row. Pull the yarn through all three of the loops. There will be three stitches in the row, two single crochets, and one single crochet decrease.

4. Chain once and turn. Then continue the next rows the same as the previous one, but decrease the number of stitches by one each time.

5. Single crochet in the first stitch of row four. Single crochet decrease, chain one, and then turn.

6. Single crochet decrease in row five, chain one, and then turn.

7. Row six is a single crochet.

8. You should now have a triangle. To finish it, fasten off your yarn and weave in the tails. Make a few of these and then link them to metal jump rings by using the jump ring tool or some needle nose pliers.

Crochet Bow

Materials

- 1 Skein yarn
- 5.0mm crochet hook or smaller

Directions

1. Chain twenty-five, half double crochet in the third chain from your hook and in every chain across.

2. For rows two through four: chain two, half double crochet in the closest stitch and in every one all the way across, and then turn.

3. Once you get to the final stitch, single crochet and cut the yarn. Pull it through and make sure it's tight, and then weave in the ends. Fold over the short ends into the middle, glue them together, and squeeze to make a bow. Then wrap some yarn around the center and glue the ends down.

Crochet Phone Cozy

Materials

- 2 Colors yarn

- Size I crochet hook

- Crochet needle

- Scissors

Directions

1. To start, chain twenty-three one color of yarn.

2. Yarn over and then double crochet in your fifth stitch back from the end that you were crocheting from. Stitch in a double crochet into every stitch to the end. There should be twenty double crochets, including your first chain three, which is your beginning double crochet.

3. For rows two through eight: Turn the yarn and chain three. Skip to the fifth stitch and double crochet to the end of the row. Keep going with the same instructions for every row until you reach the height you want.

4. To join the seams: Weave in and hide the shortest tail.

5. Fold the finished piece in half.

6. Add the needle to the longest tail end. It should be about a foot long.

7. Whipstitch the sides together and one end together. Whipstitching is threading through one side and then the other side as they line up.

8. Keep going through to the bottom with the whipstitching. Then tie a knot to hide the tail.

9. To add the top loop: Make a slip knot with the second color of yarn and add it to the hook through the top left edge of the cozy. Chain once.

10. Single crochet all the way around the edge until you reach the other side.

11. Once you're at the end, chain ten stitches.

12. Slip stitch the tenth chain through the first chain from the first color where you began. Hide the tails.

Grapefruit Coaster Pattern

Materials

- Worsted weight yarn (white and orange)
- H crochet hook
- Tapestry needle

Directions

Chain three.

1. Add nine double crochets into your first chain using the orange color. Slip stitch into the top of the first double crochet. Nine stitches total.

2. Chain two. Work two double crochet into the beginning stitch and in every stitch around. Slip stitch into the top of the first double crochet. Eighteen stitches total.

3. Chain two. Work two double crochets into the first stitch. One double crochet into the second stitch. Two double crochets into the next, one double crochet into the next

around. Slip stitch into the top of the first double crochet.

Cut your yarn and weave in the ends. Twenty-seven stitches.

4. Join the white yarn with a slip stitch. Chain once. Work two half double crochets into the first stitch and one half double crochet into the next two stitches. Two half double crochets in the next, and one double crochet in the next two stitches around. Slip stitch to the top of the first half double crochet. Then cut your yarn and weave in the ends. Thirty-six stitches total.

5. Join the white yarn using a slip stitch. Chain once. Work two single crochets into the first stitch and one single crochet in the following three stitches. Two single crochets in the next with one single crochet in the following three stitches around. Slip stitch in the top of the beginning single crochet. Cut your yarn and weave in the ends. Forty-five stitches total.

Crochet Snake

Materials

- Yarn
- Pony beads
- Tape
- Scissors

Directions

1. Finger crochet the yarn into a long chain piece around a foot long. Crochet the snake as long as you'd like.

2. When you have it as long as you'd like, begin on a second row by finger crocheting through the first chain piece. Finger crochet two to four stitches for the second row. This is going to be the snake's head.

3. Pull the yarn through the final stitch and pull it tight. Cut off the yarn about one to two inches away from the final stitch. This is going to act as the snake's tongue.

4. On the tail end of your snake, thread on three or four pony beads. With the last bead, tie a knot at the end of the tail. Tying the bead into a knot is going to help secure the beads on.

Teeny Tiny Butterfly Crochet Pattern

Materials

- Size 6 crochet hook

- Embroidery floss

Directions

1. Chain four. Slip stitch into your first stitch to make a ring.

2. Chain two. Three double crochets into a ring. Chain two. Slip stitch into the ring and repeat this entire process again.

3. Chain one. Three double crochets into a ring. Chain one. Slip stitch into the ring. Repeat this entire process once.

4. Fasten off, and make the abdomen and antennae.

Small Butterfly

1. You'll need a size 6 hook for the small butterfly. Chain four. Slip stitch into the first chain to make a ring.

2. Chain four. Three treble stitches into the ring. Chain three, slip stitch into the ring. Repeat this once.

3. Chain three. Three double crochets into the ring. Chain three, slip stitch into the ring. Repeat this once.

4. Fasten off, and make the abdomen and the antennae.

Medium Butterfly

1. Use a size C hook and chain four. Slip stitch into your first chain to make a ring.

2. Chain four times. Work three double treble stitches into the ring. Chain four, slip stitch into the ring and repeat everything in this row.

3. Chain three, work three treble crochets into a ring. Chain three, slip stitch into the ring and repeat everything once.

4. Fasten off, and make the abdomen and antennae.

Large

1. Use a size C hook and chain four. Slip stitch into the first chain and make a ring.

2. Chain four. Three treble stitches into a ring. Chain three, slip stitch into a ring and repeat everything once.

3. Chain three. Three double crochets into a ring. Chain three and slip stitch into a ring. Repeat this all once.

4. Fasten off, and make the antennae and abdomen.

Extra Large

1. Use a size G hook. Chain four and slip stitch into the first
   chain to make a ring.

2. Chain four and work three double treble crochets into a ring.
   Chain four and slip stitch into a ring. Repeat this all once.

3. Chain three, work three treble crochets into a ring. Chain
   three and slip stitch into the ring. Repeat this all once.

4. Fasten off, and make the abdomen and antennae.

Crochet Heart

Materials

- Red Worsted weight yarn

- 4.5 or size G crochet hook

Directions

1. Begin by making a magic ring.

2. Make one double crochet in the ring and make sure to work over both the ring and the tail of your yarn.

3. Make three triple crochets.

4. Then make three double crochets.

5. Then make one triple crochet to make the point of the heart.

6. Now do the other half of the heart through reversing the order of your stitches.

7. Do three double crochets.

8. Then three treble crochets.

9. Then one double crochet.

10. Pull the tail to shut your magic ring. Finish with a slip stitch. Weave in the ends and attach to a card or whatever you'd like.

Crochet Bookmark

Materials

- Yarn
- Size H crochet hook
- Crochet needle
- Scissors

Directions

1. You're going to make two circle rings, one that's small and one that's large with a chain stitch in the center. The rings are going to be crocheted just how you have the mini crochet circle rings for the first circle you make.

2. Chain four, slip stitch the hook through the first stitch in the chain to join them and make a ring. Chain one.

3. Single crochet eleven stitches into the ring.

4. When the first small circle has been made, chain thirty to forty stitches. This is going to depend on how long you want the bookmark to be or how big the book is. To be on the safe side, you can always chain a few more, forty to fifty.

5. Once you have the chain length, chain four more stitches. Bring the hook back four stitches and slip stitch it through to create a ring.

6. Chain three times. This is going to be the first double crochet.

7. Double crochet eleven to thirteen more stitches into the ring. This will depend on how thick and tight you want the circle to be.

8. Trim the yarn, pull it through, and hide the tails.

SARAH MILLER

Coffee Cozy

Materials

- Yarn
- I or size 6 crochet hook
- 28mm button
- Scissors
- Thread
- Needle

Directions

Chain ten times.

1. Single crochet in the second chain from your hook and every chain going across, and then turn. Nine single crochets total.

2. Chain one, single crochet in the first single crochet and then in every one across, turn. A total of nine single crochets. Repeat this row until the piece reaches about eight and three-quarters of an inch.

3. Slip stitch in the first four single crochets, chain six, skip the
    fifth single crochet and slip stitch in the final four single
    crochets.

4. To make the border, begin with two single crochets in the
    corner stitch, single crochet along the entire edge evenly until
    you've reached the corner.

5. Two single crochets in the corner stitch, single crochet along
    the short edge.

6. One single crochet in the bottom corner and in each stitch
    until you reach the last corner.

7. Single crochet once in that corner and in the first three slip
    stitches, and then slip stitch in the fourth single crochet.

8. Slip stitch in every chain of the button loop. Slip stitch in the
    next slip stitch, and single crochet in the final three stitches.

9. Join, cut and tuck in the ends.

10. Sew the button in place.

Scalloped Headband

Materials

- 5.00mm or size H crochet hook
- 8-Ply yarn (50 grams)
- Tapestry needle
- Scissors

Directions

1. Begin by taking the crochet hook and making a slip knot, and then crocheting seventy-one chains.

2. Chain two, crochet one-half double crochet in the following chain. Then crochet in one half double crochet for every chain across.

3. Once you've done the last row, chain one. Then single crochet all around the headband.

4. Once you reach the corners, single crochet, chain one, and then single crochet into the same stitch.

5. Begin by attaching the yarn to the first stitch along the length of the headband for the scalloped edge.

6. Chain one, and then single crochet in the same stitch. Skip one stitch before you do five double crochets in the following stitch. Skip a stitch and then crochet a single crochet. * Skip one stitch before you crochet five double crochets. Skip a stitch, and then crochet a single crochet. Repeat from the asterisk across, and be sure to end with a single crochet.

7. Fasten it off and weave in the loose ends.

8. Repeat the scalloped edging pattern on the opposite side of the headband.

9. Once you're done with the rows, connect the ends of the band together and make a circle. Slip stitch them together. Once it's together, fold the stitched parts toward the inside. Fasten it off and weave in your loose ends.

Hand Warmers

Materials

- Yarn

- Size I crochet hook

- Crochet needle

- Scissors

Directions

1. Chain stitch twenty-three times.

2. For the first row, double crochet into the fifth chain from your end. Continue to double crochet to the end of the chain. There will be a total of twenty double crochet stitches. Turn and chain three times.

3. For row two through eight, repeat row one. If you want your hand warmers to be longer on your arm, then continue to double crochet a few more rows. You have to do this according to the size you'd like.

4. Weave in and hide the shortest tail.

5. Fold the finished piece in half.

6. Add the crochet needle to the longest tail end.

7. Whipstitch the sides together two-thirds of the way up the side. To do this, thread through one side and then the other as the sides line up.

8. Leave a hole about one to two inches long and then continue to stitch up to the top. For the hole, stitch the thread through only one side and begin again where you'd like. This is going to be the thumb hole.

9. Tie a knot and hide the tail.

Stars

Materials

- Yarn
- Crochet hook that matches your yarn size
- Darning needle

Directions

1. Begin by making a magic loop. Chain three, do three double crochets, and chain one into a magic loop to form the first cluster.

2. Then do three double crochets, chain one, and repeat this four times. Slip stitch into the third chain from your beginning and then chain three.

3. Pull your magic loop tight.

4. There should now be a small pentagon made with five clusters of double crochets with a chain between each cluster.

5. Now chain five.

6. Single crochet into the second chain from the hook.

7. Half double crochet into the following chain.

8. Double crochet into the following chain.

9. Triple crochet into the following chain.

10. Slip stitch into the following chain, one space.

11. Repeat from step five for a total of five times.

12. To fast4en off, make one chain, cut off the yarn and leave a three-inch tail. Pull out the loop with the hook. Give a good tug to tighten your chain.

13. If you want to sew in the ends, you can, or you can make a simple border for your star.

14. To make the border, pick out another color and knot the new color together with your bind off tail from your star, as close to the bind off as you can get. Now slip stitch around the star.

15. Put the hook through the back loop of the first slip stitch to the left of your knot and then pull the new color through. Slip stitch around up through all five chains.

16. Once you've reached the top, chain one.

17. Now slip stitch through the back loops of your stitches. Repeat around the star and remember to make a chain one when you get to the top of the point so that the star remains pointy.

18. Once you work your way around, slip stitch into the first slip stitch of the round.

19. Use the darning needle to hide your tail.

21 Amazing Tips and Tricks for Crochet Patterns, Stitches, Hats, Bags, Flowers, Gifts, Gloves, Scarves, and Babies

Baby Blanket

Materials

- Two skeins yarn
- 5.5mm or Size I crochet hook
- Tapestry needle
- Scissors

Directions

1. Chain stitch fifty to fifty-five stitches very loosely. Make sure you maintain an even tightness so that every chain stitch is evenly spaced. This row is going to be the foundation of the blanket, so you should make it as long or as short as you'd like the blanket to be.

2. Double crochet in every chain across.

3. Repeat row two until the blanket is sixteen inches across, about twenty to twenty-four rows.

4. For the border, you can incorporate a contrasting yarn or you can use the same color. Do two double crochets for every stitch.

5. Fasten off the yarn and weave in the ends with the tapestry

   needle.

Cozy Cowl

Materials

- 1 Skein chunky yarn
- Size N crochet hook
- Crochet needle
- Scissors

Directions

1. Chain forty-five stitches.
2. Once you get to the end of the chain, straighten out the chain so that there are no twists and slip stitch through the first chain.
3. Chain three times.
4. For round one: double crochet into the fifth stitch from your hook, including the chain three. Keep going with double crochets in every stitch in the round.
5. Once you get to the end of the round, slip stitch up through to the top of the beginning chain of three in this round to join your circle.

6. For rounds three through eight: Repeat steps three through five for every round until you get to the height you prefer.

7. Once the cowl is the height you prefer, tie off the end, trim, and then hide the tails with the crochet needle.

Hacky Sack

Materials

- Worsted weight yarn
- Size H crochet hook
- Dry beans
- Stitch marker
- Scissors

Directions

1. Make the found with six stitches with the magic ring method. Put a stitch marker at the start of the round and move it to the first stitch of every round as you crochet.

2. Two single crochets in every stitch around for a total of twelve stitches.

3. Two single crochets in the following stitch, single crochet in the following stitch for eighteen stitches total around.

4. Two single crochet in the following stitch, single crochet in the next two stitches around for a total of twenty-four stitches.

5. Two single crochets in the next stitch, single crochet in the next three stitches around for a total of thirty stitches.

6. For rounds six through thirteen: single crochet around for a total of thirty stitches.

7. For round fourteen: single crochet two together, single crochet in the following three stitches around for a total of twenty-four stitches.

8. Begin filling with the beans filling.

9. For round fifteen: single crochet two together, single crochet in the following two stitches around for a total of eighteen stitches.

10. For round sixteen: single crochet two together, single crochet in the following stitch around for a total of twelve stitches.

11. If you need to, top off the stuffing at this point.

12. For round seventeen: single crochet two together until the open end has closed enough for you to tie it off. Weave in the ends and hide your tails inside the ball.

Boot Cuffs

Materials

- Sport weight yarn
- 4mm or Size G crochet hook

Directions

Chain thirteen.

1. Row One: Make a single crochet in the second chain from your hook and in all the chains going across. Chain one and turn.

2. Row Two: Single crochet in the back loop only of every single crochet. Chain one and turn.

3. For Rows Three through Forty-Four: Repeat row two and single crochet in back loop only across the row. Chain one. After four rows, you'll see the ridges of the ribbing beginning. You're halfway there at this point. After you complete row forty-four, the ribbing should be around ten inches long. Fold it so that the two edges line up. Slip stitch those two edges

together. There will now be a ring of ribbing. Now continue working around that ring.

4. Single crochet around your ring, making one single crochet in every valley. Join this with a slip stitch, and to being single crocheting put a stitch marker to mark the beginning of your round.

5. Chain one, skip one stitch, single crocheting in the following stitch, and repeat around the ring.

6. Chain one, single crochet in the chain one space, and repeat around.

7. You're not making a single crochet in between the two single crochets in the row beneath.

8. Repeat number six until the work measures around five inches tall.

9. There isn't any need to join the ends of the rounds, but you could use a stitch marker so that you know where every round ends. Fasten off and weave in the ends.

Ruffles Scarf

Materials

- 1 skein ruffle yarn

- Size I crochet hook

- Crochet stitch markers

Directions

1. Begin by stretching out the yarn a foot or two in length. The bottom of the stretched yarn will have a thicker edge. That's the outside fantasy part of the scarf. The top side will have smaller holes for loops.

2. Fold over the beginning edge of the yarn about four to five inches and line up the holes that match. Add the hook to the first hole of the folded edge. This is going to hide the end. The scarf will be thick enough with the ruffles that it is going to get lost.

3. Weave the hook into every hole and keep the yarn on the hook. There are some options here. You can weave as

minimal or as many as you want. It all depends on the fluff of the ruffled edge of the finished scarf.

4. Weave through nine holes and then stop.

5. Turn the hook and 'hook' the last loop that you went through. Pull that loop through all the other nine loops. This is your first set of gathered loops to make the ruffle.

6. This is a good time to add a stitch marker because you might lose your hook and will all unravel.

7. Continue to weave through the remainder of the yarn through every other hole of your nine loops. Gather them up and pull them through.

8. Once you come to the length you'd like or the end of your skein, then leave four to five inches unweaved.

9. To tie off the end you now have two options:

   a. You can take the end and tie a knot in it. Once the scar has fluffed around, the knot is going to disappear.

   b. You can take the final four inches of the yarn and pull them through the last hooked loop. Pull them through for around three to four inches. It should be almost doubled over itself. The end is going to get

lost in the ruffles.

Baby Booties

Materials

- 1 oz. baby sport yarn

- 5.00mm or Size H crochet hook

Directions

To begin at the toe, chain four, slip stitch in the first chain to
make a ring.

1. (Right side) Working over the tail of your yarn, chain two,
    work nine double crochets into a ring, join with a slip stitch
    in the first double crochet. Pull the end of the yarn tail to
    close up your hole. Nine stitches total.

2. Chain two, turn, two double crochets in every stitch around,
    join with a slip stitch in the first double crochet. Eighteen
    stitches total.

3. Chain two, turn, double crochet in the base of the chain two
    (one stitch increased), double crochet in every stitch around,

join with a slip stitch in the first double crochet. Nineteen stitches total.

4. Repeat round three for a total of twenty stitches.

5. Repeat round three for a total of twenty-one stitches.

6. Chain two, turn, double crochet in the following eighteen stitches. Don't work the last three stitches.

7. For rounds seven through nine: Chain two, turn, double crochet in every stitch. Eighteen stitches. Cut the yarn at the end of row nine to leave a length to sew back the seam. With the right sides together, sew the back seam. Turn the bootie right side out.

8. For the cuff, Round One: Attach the yarn with a slip stitch at the back seem of the bootie, chain two, work twenty-two double crochets evenly spaced around the top of the bootie. Join with a slip stitch in the top of the first double crochet.

9. For round two through six: Chain two, turn, double crochet in every stitch around. Join with a slip stitch in the top of the first double crochet. Round six is going to be on the outside of the bootie when the cuff is turned down.

10. For the edging: Chain one and single crochet in every stitch around. Join with a slip stitch in the first single crochet. Fasten off and weave in the ends of the yarn on the wrong side of the bootie. Turn down three rounds of the cuff.

11. Chain seventy, pull the yarn through the last stitch and pull it tight for a knot. Then pull the start end of the yarn tight for a knot. Weave tie it through with double crochet stitches of round one of the cuff. Tie a bow at the front of the bootie. Trim the ends of the yarn to about a quarter of an inch from the knot. Repeat for the second bootie.

Conclusion

Thank you for reading through this book! I hope you found some crochet projects that were of interest to you. The next step is to get started crocheting your first project! However, before you get out your yarn and crochet needle, be sure to read up on the stitches mentioned in this book. None of them were too complex, but knowing how to whipstitch before the project will give you the confidence to get through it correctly the first time.

If you enjoyed what you found in this book, please be sure to leave a review at your online eBook retailer's website.

Thank you for reading! - Sarah Miller

69006810R00033

Made in the USA
Lexington, KY
23 October 2017